SCENES FROM CHILDHOOD

by Mary Bruce Sharon

E. P. DUTTON   NEW YORK

For Carroll

The publisher gratefully acknowledges the following
for their kind permission to reproduce the paintings
by Mary Bruce Sharon which appear in this book:
Cincinnati Art Museum for *"Over the Rhine" on Grandpa's
Bridge*, Gift of Mr. and Mrs. Harrison P. Warrener;
Hallmark Cards Incorporated for *My Doll's Washtub*,
My Doll and I at Grandma's, and *Christmas Dinner*;
and Henrietta Sharon Aument for all other paintings.

Library of Congress Cataloging in Publication Data

Sharon, Mary Bruce, 1878–1961.   Scenes from childhood.

1. Sharon, Mary Bruce, 1878–1961.   2. Painters—
United States—Biography.   I. Title.
ND237.S467A2   1978   759.13 [B]   78-4939
ISBN: 0-525-38820-6

Published in the United States by E.P. Dutton, a Division
of Sequoia-Elsevier Publishing Company, Inc., New York

Published simultaneously in Canada by Clarke,
Irwin & Company Limited, Toronto and Vancouver

Editor: Ann Durell   Designer: Riki Levinson
Printed and bound in Hong Kong
First Edition   10 9 8 7 6 5 4 3 2 1

Introduction

My mother, Mary Bruce Sharon, whom I called Mouse, was past seventy when she began to paint. Her paintings grew out of a book of reminiscences and recipes which she started to write in 1949. During pauses while she searched for a word, she made little drawings with her pen. My husband, painter Carroll Aument, was delighted with the naive charm of the drawings. He gave her some paints and brushes and said, "Why don't you try painting?" She did, and she never stopped until she died at eighty-three, in 1961.

During the thirteen years of her career as a painter, we shielded her from exploitation and pressures. She painted what she wanted, the way she wanted—sometimes spending four months on a painting, lingering lovingly over every detail—and remaining to the end of her life a completely untaught, uninfluenced, and unspoiled primitive.

From the beginning, the critics treated her seriously. She exhibited in France and in a number of museums in the United States. During 1974-76, the Smithsonian Institution circulated a traveling exhibition of her work in the United States. The American Museum in Bath, England, presented her work in a bicentenary exhibition in 1976, and her paintings toured Europe under the sponsorship of embassies of the United States during 1976-78. Now her paintings appear in a book for the first time.

Every picture in this book tells a story. Each story illumines a certain time and way of life in America that is gone forever. The descriptions I have put together to accompany the paintings tell these stories in my mother's own words, as she told them to me.

Henrietta Bruce Sharon Aument
Kalamazoo, Michigan

Myself (1882 or '83)

   I remember this outfit that I am wearing very well. The dress was embroidered and Mama had had it made for me in New York. My bonnet came from Paris. My spring-heeled shoes were new and so was my parasol. I still have the little blue heart I was wearing. The Roman sash completed my costume, which even then, at four or five or whatever I was, I thought very chic.

My Doll's Washtub (1883)

This is a picture of me in my playroom. Mama had it decorated in pink, my favorite color. The pictures were all scenes from nursery rhymes.

My favorite toys were the washtub and stove. I washed my doll clothes in the tub, hung them out to dry, and ironed them.

The stove was real, and I cooked on it. I served meals to my dolls, and I also invited Mama and Grandpa to come to tea. My little black spaniel, Tilly, enjoyed everything I served her. I was a very domestic child, and cooking has always been one of my favorite pursuits.

My Doll and I at Grandma's (1885)

Here I am at Grandma Green's. My doll is with me. Her name was Mary Catherine. She was French, with a kid body and a bisque head.

We always wore matching outfits. They were made for us by Madame Leonie, Mama's French dressmaker in New York. I always thought Madame Leonie and Mary Catherine had a special affinity because they both came from Paris.

When Mary Catherine traveled with me, she had a little trunk for her clothes that was just like mine. I made tickets for her when we went on the train, and the conductor punched them, just like a grown-up's.

My First Pony (1886)

    Grandpa gave me my first pony. I named him Darling. The first day I rode him, he threw me. I still thought he was darling. After a period of time and many lumps of sugar, he thought I was too, and he never threw me again.

Fishing with Grandpa (1886)

Grandpa used to take me fishing with him. As I recall, there weren't many fish caught. Grandpa liked to sit on a riverbank —the Licking River, in back of his house— and recite Robert Burns, his favorite poet and a good Scotsman too. He was very proud of his Scottish heritage —he was descended from Robert Bruce.

Grandpa liked to eat the big picnic lunches we brought. He followed this by a nice long nap with his old black hat over his face.

My Father's House in Washington, Kentucky (1886)

My father was Richard Lashbrook Green. My mother was Henrietta Bruce of Covington, Kentucky. My father fell in love with my mother when he saw her picture on Grandpa's desk, and he was determined to marry her even before he met her.

It was a very happy marriage, although it was a short one. My father died when he was only twenty-five. Though she had many suitors, Mama never married again.

This is a picture of my father's house. It shows me arriving with Mama and Grandpa for a visit with Grandma Green and Aunt Ann. The little boy was a cousin.

I was the only Green grandchild, and everybody in that dear town of Washington always gave me a royal welcome. They all said, "Mary Bruce, you look just like your papa!"

My Aunt Pauline (1886)

My Aunt Pauline, Mama's eldest sister, was a great belle. When she was a young girl, she was so beautiful that all the young men for miles around came courting her. Grandpa had a sculptor come from New York to immortalize one of her beautiful arms. And for years Aunt Pauline's marble arm decorated a mantelpiece in his home.

Aunt Pauline visited Yankeeland, as she called it, when she was a young girl, and wrote home that she couldn't abide it. She said Yankees were crude, and that they served cold doughnuts and applesauce for breakfast.

Mama (1870s)

Mama was not flirtatious, so she wasn't a real belle in the sense that Aunt Pauline was, but she was very beautiful.

She was small and feminine, prone to faint and blush, very modest, and even a little shy. After Papa died I felt I had to look after her, so I worked hard to discourage all her beaus. My strategy worked. She never married anyone else and just belonged to me.

"Over the Rhine" on Grandpa's Bridge (1867)

In the 1850s, Grandpa was president pro tem of a company and pushed plans for the building of the suspension bridge between Covington, Kentucky, and Cincinnati, Ohio. He invited a young engineer named John Roebling (who had not yet built the Brooklyn Bridge, but who was already getting quite a reputation) to spend six months in his Covington home and draw up the plans for the bridge.

The reason why Grandpa had the bridge built always fascinated me. Grandpa's three younger daughters went to school in Cincinnati. They didn't like the long, cold ferry ride "over the Rhine," as they called the Ohio River, and begged him to "build us a bridge, Pa." So he did.

This painting shows the way I imagined it must have looked with Grandpa, Grandma, Aunt Pauline, Uncle James, the little girls, and their nurse making their first trip across the the new bridge.

I Visit Sitting Bull *(1885)*

When I was about seven or eight, Mama and I visited Sitting Bull. He was a prisoner on a reservation somewhere in Kansas.

I thought he looked very sad and wondered if it was because he was sitting all the time. It seemed to me if he changed his name to Running Bull he might have had a better time and maybe even escaped.

Grandpa's Escape (1863)

I don't know just what Grandpa did during the Civil War, but I suspect he was spying for the Confederacy. He seemed to have been involved with the escape of General Morgan, the Rebel Raider, from Ohio State Prison. The General's aide, Colonel Basil Duke, was a cousin-in-law of Pauline, my Mama's sister.

I have a letter that Grandpa's niece, Lucy Dorsey, wrote to him a few days after the escape. She was the only visitor General Morgan had on the afternoon of Thanksgiving, 1863—the day he got away.

A short time later, Grandpa packed his bag, bade a tearful good-bye to his family, and escaped himself, by leaving his home secretly at night. Before long, the house was surrounded by Yankee troops. Apparently Grandpa had provided the gold that Lucy Dorsey must have smuggled into the prison to aid the General in getting away.

This is the way I imagined it must have been the night Grandpa escaped.

All the Transportation in My Childhood (1885)

I always loved traveling and would go anywhere at the drop of a hat. A good many hats must have been dropped in my childhood, for I did a great deal of traveling.

I liked trains best of all. Wherever I went, I took Mary Catherine with me. There she is in her doll buggy, and there I am pushing the buggy.

Grandpa's Kitchen (1885)

Grandpa had a wonderful kitchen. There were always delicious things in it for a hungry little girl to eat.

I thought of it as "*Grandpa's* kitchen" because Grandpa loved to entertain, and the cook was prepared to serve as many as twelve unexpected guests at any meal. She always made special things for me when I was at Grandpa's, and I learned a lot about cooking from her.

That's one of my dolls in the chair beside me, and Grandpa's pug dog, whose name was Robert Burns. Everyone called him Bobby.

Christmas Dinner (1885)

Christmas at Grandpa's was the high point of the year. There was so much excitement, so many presents, such delicious food, so many fond relatives. Sometimes there would be as many as fifty of the Bruce cousins to help celebrate, but Grandpa told me he loved me best. He was the only father I ever really knew.

Dinner was usually in the middle of the day. Roast turkey, stuffed goose, ham aged in Grandpa's smokehouse, hot rolls, hot biscuits, sweet potatoes, white potatoes, preserves and jellies and, of course, mince pies, sweet potato pies, white and dark fruit-cakes, all kinds of other delectable desserts, nuts and raisins, and brandy for the gentlemen. No wonder all the grown-ups took naps afterward, while the children played with their new toys.

In the evening, everyone revived enough to partake largely of a cold collation, preceded by several toddies. Later on, Grandpa would resort to his "faithful friend," bicarbonate of soda.

The Arkansas Traveler (1886)

Grandpa went to Eureka Springs to drink the waters for his health. He took Mama and me along. I learned to play the "Arkansas Traveler" on the banjo to please him.

Grandpa entertained the minister with mint juleps. When the minister didn't come home, his wife was worried. She found him sleeping in one of the gullies that ran underneath the sidewalks of Eureka. Grandpa said he was the only man he'd ever heard of who fell below the gutter.

My First Visit to the Kentucky Derby
(1886)

I was about eight years old when I first attended the Kentucky Derby. I went with Mama and Grandpa in a cousin's tallyho (I'm the little girl in pink on top).

Bruce relations came from all over Kentucky: from Paris, Lexington, Maysville, Washington, Flemingsburg. I remember the excitement, the gaily dressed crowds, the beautiful horses, the delicious picnic lunch we had, and the band playing "My Old Kentucky Home."

Most of all, I remember the horse, owned by a cousin, that sat down and refused to budge, and how I broke down and cried while the grown-ups just had another mint julep.

Coming Out of Church in New York City (1886)

Mama and I spent part of every year in New York. We both loved the city—I still do.

Mama had lived in New York for several years when she was a little girl. She went to school at Madame Mears, 222 Madison Avenue.

My First Visit to the Metropolitan Museum (1885)

I first visited the Metropolitan Museum when I was about seven years old. I went with Mama and Grandpa.

We were staying at the old Brevoort Hotel where Mama had spent part of her honeymoon. It took a long time to get way uptown in a carriage from the Brevoort to the Metropolitan.

Grandpa was very interested in art, and Mama collected paintings. I thought the museum was very beautiful, but I had to admit to Mama that I really preferred a toy store.

The Metropolitan and I are about the same age, but the Metropolitan is better preserved.

I Go to the Circus (1886)

Every summer I went to the circus with Grandpa. He loved circuses as much as I did. We always sat in the front row and ate peanuts and drank lemonade.

I liked the elephants best, but Grandpa preferred the circus people. He seemed to know all of them, and after the performance he always took me around and introduced me. I met Buffalo Bill, who seemed to be a friend of Grandpa's.

I met Tom Thumb and his wife, too. They were even smaller than I was. They invited me to join the circus and travel with them, and I was wild to do it, but Grandpa told me I'd better wait until I was grown up.

I've put Buffalo Bill and Tom Thumb and his wife in this painting.

The title display is set in Erbar Initials photo-lettering, and the other display and text in Goudy Oldstyle Alphatype.